Minibeasties and Their ADVENTURES

2: Celine the Centipede

Chris Hames

AuthorHouse™ UK
1663 Liberty Drive
Bloomington, IN 47403 USA
www.authorhouse.co.uk
Phone: 0800.197.4150

Published by AuthorHouse 11/09/2018

ISBN: 978-1-7283-8023-0 (sc)
ISBN: 978-1-7283-8024-7 (e)

authorHOUSE®

Minibeasties and Their ADVENTURES

2: Celine the Centipede

Dear Parents/Guardians,
Welcome to book 2 from the world of Minibeasties!

This series of booklets is intended to entertain children while providing a positive learning experience. I hope that you will find the books informative and helpful in the development of literacy and numeracy skills. While introducing elements of science alongside social awareness, they provide a range of activities to engage the child's imagination and enhance comprehension skills.

QR codes are included to provide links to more information about the animals.

Please send feedback and or suggestions to Chris via minibeasties20@aol.com

Thank you to Isabelle Williams, age 9, for drawing the trees on page 3 and to Sarah Taylor for assistance with collating and proof-reading.

3

Celine lives in the forest. She likes to explore the forest floor.

4

Celine likes to rest in small spaces under stones, and amongst leaves or wood.

6

Celine likes to eat smaller animals – she is a carnivore. She likes to hunt amongst leaf litter.

9

Celine has a lot of legs. She has a pair of legs attached to each segment of her body. This means she has seventy seven (77) pairs of legs, which means she has seventy seven lots of two legs (77 x 2), making one hundred and fifty four (154) legs altogether!

11

Celine's friend Celeste is a different type of centipede with 21 pairs of legs, which means that Celeste has twenty one lots of two (21 x 2) legs, making 42 legs altogether.

13

Celine will grow to be seven (7) centimetres long. She has a yellow coloured outer skeleton to protect herself.

15

Celine has Company

- a short story.

One sunny summer's day, Celine was enjoying a comfortable rest under her favourite stone.

It was a shiny smooth stone lying among some logs and leaves, and it was usually very peaceful there. Celine was just settling to sleep when she felt something move the stone. She woke up with a shock and called out "Who's there?"

"Why?" came a gruff reply.

"This is my stone!" said Celine.

"Oh, well, can I come and rest for a while?" asked the stranger.

Celine did not want to share her special space with anyone she did not know. She asked; "Who are you and why do you want to be here?"

"Oh, I should have said, my name is Cameron – your friend Celeste said that I could rest under your stone because it is large, and she said that it is safe to stay with you."

"Well," replied Celine, "if Celeste said that you could join me, come in Cameron and make yourself at home."

Soon, a rather large and round head pushed its way under the stone, followed by a big, long and soft body. Cameron was a caterpillar!

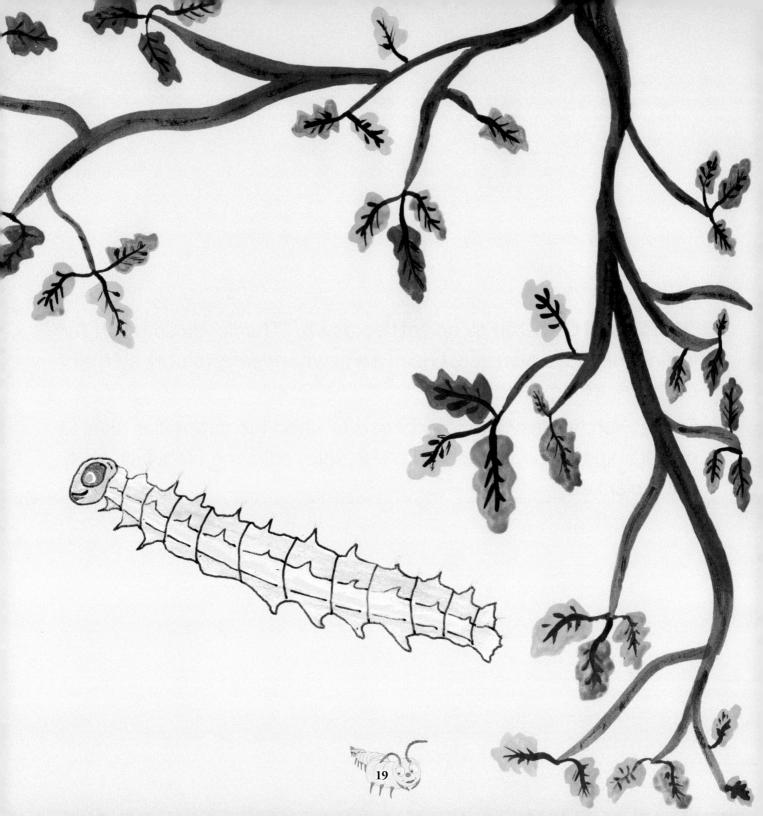

"Hello." said Cameron as he settled down, "Thank you so much for letting me stay.... you see, I need somewhere safe to stay so that I can have a long sleep."

Celine watched as Cameron began to shed his caterpillar skin to reveal a special cocoon, called a chrysalis, covering his whole body like a blanket.

21

He went to sleep. Cameron slept for a long, long time.

Celine began to worry about the caterpillar because whenever she went out to find food and to get some exercise, she would come back to find that Cameron was still snugly wrapped in his chrysalis. He had stopped snoring.

One day, Celine came back from a long walk to find that Cameron had at last woken up. At first she was a little confused, because she did not recognise her new friend, but then she realised what had happened.

Celine was very excited to see that Cameron had changed into a most handsome butterfly, full of bright colours and almost ready to fly up into the sky!

"Oh, I need to stretch!" Cameron announced as he walked carefully out from the stone on his new legs and began to spread his delicate new wings. Celine watched as the most beautiful wings unfolded and shimmered in the sun. They fluttered and she could see that Cameron was eager to try them out. Soon, he flew gently away. "Goodbye Celine," he called from above, "Thank you for sharing your stone with me – I'll look out for some little insects for you while I'm flying around!"

23

Celine went back to the stone to have a sleep, pleased that she had her special place to herself again. She was just dozing off when she heard a voice, "Hi Celine, how are you? Did Cameron come to visit you?" It was her best friend Celeste who had come to see her. Celine did not mind being woken up and she told Celeste all about her meeting with Cameron and his amazing change into the butterfly flying above.

Colour in Celine's picture

Can you add her legs and antennae?

<u>Quiz!</u>

Where does Celine live?

_____

What does she like to do?

_____

What does Celine eat?

_____

How many legs does she have?

_____

What colour is she?

_____

How long is she?

_____

28

Celine's Wordsearch

```
C Z A W P D X W C
B A Q C J B S E E
C S T A G A T B L
O J Z M L O O S E
A A C E L I N E S
N E T R A P E E T
D Y C O C O O N E
A M S N R E A M E
```

Can you find these words in the grid? **CELINE, CAMERON, CELESTE, STONE, COCOON**

Poem

Celine was under her favourite stone,
and soon discovered she was not alone;
for she had a visitor,
a great big caterpillar...
who became a butterfly and then was gone!

Cloze Passage

Can you find the correct places
to put the missing words?

Celine and Celeste are .... Celine wanted to rest under a .... but found she was not ....

Cameron joined her while he was a .... and he left after he had changed into a ....

(centipedes, caterpillar, stone, alone, butterfly)

33

Find out more about Celine's family...

34

Celine's Wordsearch - ANSWERS

```
C Z A W P D X W C
B A Q C J B S E E
C S T A G A T B L
O J Z M L O O S E
A A C E L I N E S
N E T R A P E E T
D Y C O C O O N E
A M S N R E A M E
```

CELINE, CAMERON, CELESTE, STONE, COCOON

Printed in the United States
By Bookmasters